The Life and Adventures of Monica Monarch

by
Jules Poirier

Master Books

First printing: January 1998

ISBN: 0-89051-189-6
Library of Congress Number: 97-73933

Cover by Janell Robertson
Cover art by Ron Hight
Interior cartoons by Norm Daniels

Printed in the United States of America.

Acknowledgments

I am indebted to many who have written before me and to those who have contributed their knowledge and suggestions to me. I want especially to thank Dr. Robert E. Kofahl for his scientific survey of the book. I'd like to thank two grammar school teachers, Mrs. Athalie Okken, a first grade teacher, and Mrs. Sandi Bennett, a sixth grade teacher, for their suggestions and approval and encouragement to publish the book.

Thanks to artist Mr. Norm Daniels for drawing the black and white cartoons which made the book more enjoyable for everyone to read, and to Mr. Clayton Jerome Clark III for doing the scientific black and white drawings.

My appreciation to Mr. Robert J. Allen of the Gulf Coast Research Laboratory in Ocean Springs, Mississippi, for taking pictures of the monarch butterfly forelegs and eye with a scanning electron microscope (SEM).

Finally, I thank my dear wife, Hazel, for her suggestions which added spice to the stories, and who helped me raise the monarchs and whose patience and encouragement enabled me to finish this book.

— Jules Poirier

Dedication

This book is dedicated to our God and Saviour, the great Designer and Creator of all to His children whom He created and especially to those whose inquiry into the complex designs of God's creatures will bring them into a greater and stronger faith in the God of creation than ever before.

Introduction

The monarch butterfly is such a beautiful, complex, and interesting design I felt I should write a book about this beautiful flying machine that only God could have made. Random chance could never have designed and created a monarch butterfly. Therefore, I wrote my first book about the details of the design of the monarch butterfly. The book was called *From Darkness to Light to Flight* because the caterpillar goes into the chrysalis totally blind and in 60 seconds becomes a beautiful green chrysalis with 36 brilliant gold spots on its surface. About eight days later it comes out of the chrysalis seeing all the colors of the rainbow including ultraviolet. Within about two hours it is able to fly as far as 3,000 miles away to a place it has never seen, to the same tree its parents had migrated to in the neo-volcanic mountains west of Mexico City.

After finishing the adult book, many people asked me to write one for children. Therefore I have written this book, *The Life and Adventures of Monica the Monarch Butterfly*. Monica tells of her adventures as she travels from Nova Scotia, Canada, to Mexico. This round trip journey covers a distance of 6,000 miles and Monica has many exciting experiences as she travels this long journey. I hope you enjoy this book. It has scientific information about the monarch inserted in the pages of the adventure so you can learn important facts about the monarch butterfly.

Hello, how are you?

I hope it's a good day for you and that you are feeling well and happy and enjoying the life that God has given you. My name is Monica. I am a monarch butterfly. You must like butterflies or you wouldn't be reading this book. I have a wonderful life and I would like to tell you about all my exciting adventures and how I got my name.

All monarchs are very unique in that we don't start our lives as a beautiful orange, black, and white creature that can fly. When you were born you were a tiny helpless baby. However, as you grew you simply got bigger. Not so with monarchs. We actually go through four stages. It is called a life cycle. The four stages are egg, caterpillar, chrysalis (pupa), and butterfly. I started out as a tiny egg, then three days later I came out of the egg as a caterpillar. Twenty days later I was transformed into a beautiful green and gold-colored chrysalis. After eight days inside the chrysalis I was changed into a butterfly.

We butterflies are lucky as we are one of God's loveliest creatures. Even though we look delicate and soft, we can be very tough and endure many hardships, as you will soon learn. I invite you to join me in the adventure of my life. Come fly with me over the tall mountains and see God's beauty below. Come play with me in the warm summer meadows. Be my friend

A chrysalis is the name given to the pupa of a butterfly. The pupa of the moth is called a cocoon. All chrysalises have some gold colors on them. The Greek word *chrysalis* means the gold colored pupa of a butterfly. Cocoons are usually gray or black and are made of silk that certain insect larvae spin about themselves before the pupa stage begins. The chrysalis is what is left over after the larva sheds its outer skin, eyes, spinning machine, and 16 legs.

and have a look into the special lives of monarch butterflies.

My life, inside an egg,

started when I was born on September 1 in Halifax, Nova Scotia, Canada. While living there I completed my four life-cycle changes in 30 days. On October 1, I felt led to start traveling 3,000 miles to the beautiful high, tree-covered mountains west of Mexico City where my parents and my grandparents went every winter to rest and enjoy themselves. On the trip to Mexico I had many adventures and almost died several times, but God saved my life each time. I wintered in Mexico for four months, then returned a year later to Nova Scotia, Canada, on September 1, to the same place where I was born. I hope you enjoy reading about my adventures as I travel this 6,000 mile round-trip journey.

My Birth!

September 1

was a very special day! It was the day I was born. This is how it all began. First, my mother looked for a nice place for me to live. She searched for a green leaf of a milkweed plant on which to attach my egg (see pictures below). Mom knew that when I became a caterpillar, I could only eat milkweed leaves. I would get sick if I ate any other plant. Most other insects and animals become sick eating the milkweed plant, so God seems to have made the many kinds of milkweed plants, in most parts of the world, mainly for us monarch butterflies.

Mom knew the most

tasty milkweed leaves grew near the streams flowing with running water. She finally found one of the plants near Indian Creek, Nova Scotia. She looked all over the leaf to make sure that no other harmful insects, such as spiders, aphids, or ants were on the leaf. Mom made sure no other monarch egg was on the leaf because there wasn't enough food

Top view of 1-day-old egg, magnified x 35.

Side view of 1-day-old egg, magnified x 31.

Details of single needle, magnified x 740.

for two baby caterpillars to eat. The fact that she could see a tiny pinhead-sized egg means my mother had very good eyes.

Before my mother could attach me to a milkweed leaf, she also had to be sure that its food was good enough for me to survive on as a caterpillar. Mom had a special way of testing it. She could tell if the milkweed leaf's food was good by pushing

six, sharp, small needles on the end of her two forelegs, deep into the surface of the leaf.

Tip of male foreleg, magnified x 78.

Butterfly antenna showing red smell sensor at tip, magnified x 24.

Mom then lowered her two antennas and smelled the juices with the two smelling sensors on the tip of her antennas. Her smelling sensors are 2,000 times more sensitive than your nose. Then she tasted the juices with the four taste sensors on the bottom of her other four large feet. If the leaf juices smelled and tasted good, she would glue my egg to the bottom of the leaf. If not, she would fly to another leaf.

The two male hairy forelegs have no needles on them because they don't lay eggs and have no need for the needles. They use their forelegs for balancing themselves during mating.

Male (top) mating with female, magnified x 1.25.

Before my mother could attach my egg to a leaf, several wonderful things had to happen. First, she made an egg for me to live in. It had 20 vertical lines and 500 circular chain-like structures holding it together. At the top of the egg there was a hole. This hole was important so the male sperm could enter it just when Mother wanted me to be born. She stored sperm in one pouch in her body and some eggs in another pouch. When mother wanted me to be born she selected one egg for me to live in and sent it out of the pouch and into a long tube called the oviduct. Then she let one sperm out of its pouch and sent the sperm into the same oviduct. The tiny sperm, smaller than the hole in the top of my egg, would wiggle itself along the oviduct until it reached the egg. Then the sperm propelled itself through the hole getting inside my egg. As the egg and sperm, now together, left the tube, my mother put a drop of powerful glue on the bottom of the egg and glued it to the bottom of the milkweed leaf. This is how I was born. Isn't this a wonderful birth process? You were born in a similar way. Your father's sperm entered your mother's egg which started your birth process and nine months later you were born as a wonderful baby. Aren't you glad you were born so you could enjoy all the wonderful things God created for us to see and experience?

As time went on, the living sperm combined with the new egg to make me into a living embryo, or baby. I began to grow inside the egg. I developed a heart, a head capsule with a miniature sewing machine and

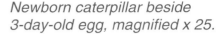

Tiny caterpillar emerging from 3-day-old egg, magnified x 21.

six eye lenses, 16 legs, stomach, and other organs.

After about 3 days I had developed into a baby caterpillar (see pictures above). I could see a foggy white light shining through the clear transparent egg. I could only see black and white light with my simple eyes. All of this being born business made me hungry so I began eating the yoke materials that were for me inside my egg. I ate and ate and finally, I ate a hole right through the wall of the egg. Now the light was shining brightly through this hole! As I ate more of the egg I noticed my body could get through the large hole. This was the break I'd been waiting for! I crawled out of the hole and onto the milkweed leaf. *Boy, I said to myself, Where am I? What a beautiful place!* Standing up on my ten suction-cup footed prolegs, I swayed back and forth looking at my surroundings. I wondered how big the world was that I had just entered.

Then I heard, or sensed, a strange sound. I saw a tall, strange-looking creature. It was a boy, about 15 years old. What was I supposed to do? He was holding a black box and pointing it in my direction. I decided to go about my business and pretend he wasn't there. Maybe he would just go away. Very gently and quietly I heard him say: "What a cute little monarch caterpillar you are. I will call you Monica." I quickly stopped moving because I was afraid he might hurt me. I stood still for about one minute waiting for him to move. When he didn't move, I again began to ignore him. Finally, a little frustrated, he said, "Monica you must be able to hear me because you stopped moving when I spoke. I only want to be your friend. My name is Joe. I live in the farmhouse over the hill. I know all about monarch butterflies because my mother and I have read many books about them. You've just hatched out of your egg and become a lovely caterpillar. That's why I took your picture. I already have one of you attached to the milkweed plant. Please Monica, can't you trust me"?" Joe seemed nice. He could have hurt me, but he didn't. Maybe we could be friends!

I was still hungry so I ate the rest of my egg. My black head was made of a strong material called chitin, something like the material of your fingernail. My black head capsule had 3 eyes on both the left side and the right side. It also had something like a miniature sewing machine on the front of the head capsule. The sewing machine had a spinneret or hollow tube from which a liquid from my silk gland could be squirted in a thin stream. In about 2 seconds this liquid dried into a strong white silky cord. I could make silky webs like a spider by moving my head back and forth, using my two little arms under my head to weave the pattern I wanted. Sometimes I would make silk ladders to climb on slick or smooth walls.

Head capsule of 14-day-old caterpillar, magnified x 17.

After about six days, I was eating so much milkweed that my outer skin was feeling tight around my inner body. I was about ready to bust! I knew I had to remove my outer skin and make room for a new larger one to grow over my body.

The caterpillar is 16 days old, magnified 1.81 times.

Therefore, I spun a silk pad with my miniature sewing machine. Then I attached my two rear prolegs to the silk pad I had just made. I spun another silk pad in front of my head. Then I took my 3 pairs of front legs, with claws on them, and used them to pull myself out of my outer skin.

Now I proceeded to take the head capsule off my head, with my three front legs, and threw it away (see below). This resulted in my becoming almost blind, because my six lenses for my eyes were on my head capsule! I waited patiently for several hours and then my new skin and new head capsule begin to grow over my internal body. This process is known as molting. I did this 4 times in a period of 20 days. Each time I molted I became bigger and bigger until I weighed 1.5 grams which was 2,700 times more than when I was first born! By now, I was about 2 inches long. My outer skin colors formed a pattern of yellow, black, and white rings. My head capsule was black as coal.

Monica removing head capsule.

Joe was watching me grow during those days and took some photos of my growth. Joe told his mother all about me and she marveled how wonderfully monarchs are made. Joe said, "Mother I mea- sured Monica's heartbeat today. It's about 60 beats per minute. I can see her rear skin moving up and down in rhythm with her heart beat. At times it beats fast when she thinks someone is going to hurt her."

My Transformation from a Caterpillar to a Chrysalis

By now I was 20 days old and considered myself to be a full-grown adult monarch caterpillar. I was eating night and day and enjoying every minute of it. Then one day a mouse saw me. I could tell by the look on his face that he wanted to eat me! He had a vicious snarl on his lips and he was licking them hungrily! This guy meant business and I didn't plan on sticking around long enough to argue that I wasn't a good meal choice.

When I saw him coming towards me, naturally I was scared to death and suddenly let loose of the milkweed. I curled up into a ball, fell to the ground, and was suddenly surrounded by tall grass. Mr. Mean Mouse looked for me, but he couldn't find me because I was hidden. I also stayed very still and didn't move. All this time I was remembering Psalm 23 that Joe taught me. I kept thinking about David when he said, "I will fear no evil: for thou art with me." Have you ever been scared and thought of those words? After about 15 minutes he gave up looking for me and left.

When I decided it was safe, I climbed back up the milkweed plant to finish my delicious meal of leaves. However, I was beginning to lose my appetite. The milkweed just didn't look so tasty anymore. My tummy felt funny. Somehow I knew I was about to start another change, the most exciting and amazing part of my life cycle. I instinctively realized I had to get ready so I

Mouse sees lunch!

began looking for a good place to build the final silk pad to which I would attach myself. I wanted to become a butterfly and get away from this earthly life. That was the reason for my being born. I knew I needed to find a place under a log or tree limb protected from rain, wind, and the view of enemy creatures. I would be virtually helpless during this time, and could not escape enemies.

I finally found a nice place under a log near Joe's home. I made the silk pad in about an hour and then fastened my two rear prolegs to it. Then I hung my head down so that my caterpillar body looked like the letter "J." I felt funny inside my body. I had no desire to eat. My body was experiencing some major changes. I could feel my stomach and intestines dissolving. Almost all of my insides were disappearing,

The caterpillar is 20 days old and hanging in a J-shape, magnified x 1.

except for my heart and wing cells in the inner surface of my outer shell.

I was beginning to feel alone and scared when I heard the voice of my best friend, Joe. He said, "Don't worry, Monica, God loves you and so do I. Listen to what His Word says in Isaiah 43:7: "Even every one that is called by my name; for I have created him for my glory, I have formed him; yea, I have made him.' You see Monica, you are a very important part of God's planned creation. Have faith that you will become a new creature in God, just as I did when I gave Jesus my life." Those words were a comfort to me during this time of great change. Just to think that the Creator cared about me and that I was part of His great plan made me feel cared for and special. You are part of this also, even more than butterflies!

After 12 hours of these strange events inside me, I saw the light of the rising sun. I knew I must act quickly or my strength would be gone. I took a deep breath and began expanding my muscles until the skin behind my head broke in two. Then I began jerking up and down so that my head, 16 old legs, and outer skin began moving upward in jerks at two-second intervals. After 48 seconds my head capsule, 16 legs, and old skin were all at the top near the silk pad. I could not see a thing because I had removed my head capsule carrying the lenses for my eyes.

At this time, I moved my cremaster (a small 0.1 inch long black rod) attached to the end of my abdomen up through a hole in my outer skin. I tried hard to push its tip with hundreds of microscopic hooks into the silk pad. I knew that unless I attached my cremaster to the pad, my body would fall to the ground and I would die. The rear prolegs were temporary suction cup-like legs and they would soon dry up and fall off. Therefore, I lunged my cremaster forward toward the silk pad for the third time with all my strength. Finally, I could feel it hit the silk pad. To insure that the cremaster was securely fastened to the pad I rotated my body clockwise three times burying the cremaster hooks deeper into the silk pad. Now I felt relieved because my body was securely fastened to the pad. I must now remove the old skin and head capsule from the pad or else it might touch my outer soft shell and distort my future wings, and I wouldn't be able to fly. So I jerked violently back and forth and sideways until I felt the old skin fall to the ground below.

In 60 seconds I had been transformed from a caterpillar to a beautiful

Cremaster of chrysalis, magnified x 33.

Caterpillar's skin, discarded after 60 seconds, magnified x 16.

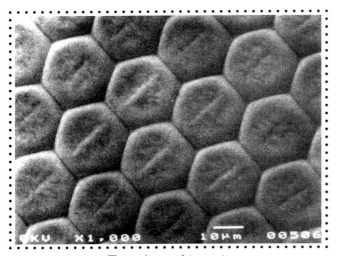

Top view of twenty
six-sided lenses of eye, magnified x 818.

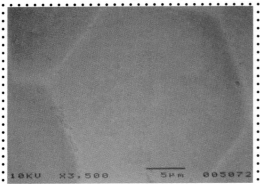

Six-sided lens, magnified x 2083.

green chrysalis. Joe could hardly believe what his eyes were seeing! It had happened so fast! He took some photos of this transformation which you can see on this page. Note the 24 metallic-like gold spots near the top part of the chrysalis. Joe called these 24 gold spots the gold crown because they looked like a king's gold crown. Inside the gold crown is my heart, beating at about 60 beats per minute. Below it the inside of my chrysalis was turning into a green liquid except for my wing cells within the first outer 0.05 inches of my outer shell. I could feel these changes taking place but I had no control over them. Some higher force had designed me to become a butterfly. I could hardly wait! It

16

After 2 seconds.

After 4 seconds.

After 22 seconds.

After 36 seconds.

After 38 seconds.

After 48 seconds.

Chrysalis, one day old.

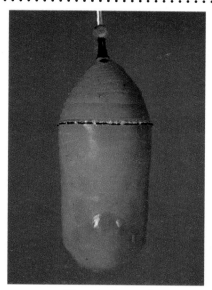

Front view of
4-day-old pupa.

Front view of
7-day-old pupa.

Right side of
7-day-old pupa.

Rear view of
7-day-old pupa.

Front view of
8-day-old pupa.

Chrysalis pictures magnified x 2.5.

was wonderful to feel my wing cells growing. After being in total darkness for six days my two eyes were beginning to appear. By the seventh day two large eyes were completed. Each compound eye was made with 6,000 light sensors, each with microscopic lenses.

Chrysalis' red heart centered in the abdominal area of the gold crown, magnified x 5.

*Right side of
8-day-old pupa,
magnified x 3.8.*

*Rear view of
8-day-old pupa,
magnified x 3.8.*

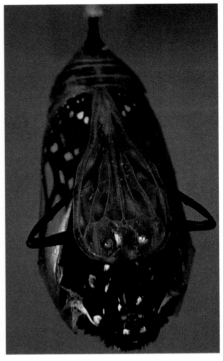

*Butterfly emerging
on eighth day,
magnified x 3.8.*

*Butterfly hanging from
shell and filling wings,
magnified x 2.*

*Butterfly with wings
fully inflated,
magnified x 1.3.*

*Empty shell of pupa,
magnified x 2.*

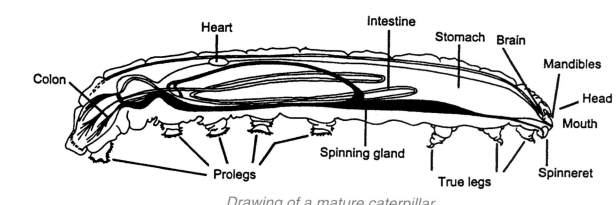

Drawing of a mature caterpillar.

Labeled parts: Heart, Intestine, Stomach, Brain, Mandibles, Head, Mouth, Spinneret, True legs, Spinning gland, Prolegs, Colon

I was now able to see all the colors of the rainbow including ultraviolet light. Ultraviolet light is from the sun and cannot be seen by humans. It is the same light that gave Joe his nice tan, but too much of an exposure can cause skin cancer in people, also.

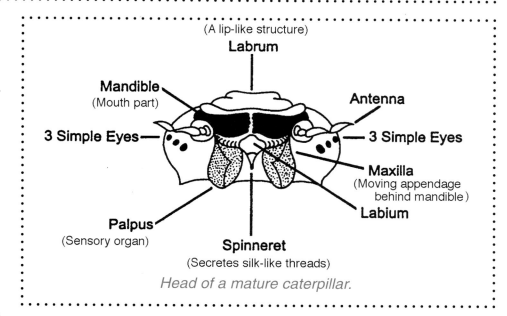

(A lip-like structure)
Labrum

Mandible
(Mouth part)

Antenna

3 Simple Eyes

3 Simple Eyes

Maxilla
(Moving appendage behind mandible)

Labium

Palpus
(Sensory organ)

Spinneret
(Secretes silk-like threads)

Head of a mature caterpillar.

I also had a navigational computer that could tell me where I was on the earth and how to get to my parent's wintering site *3,000* miles away in Mexico. I had never even seen this place! By the eighth day I had developed into a mature butterfly. I thought to myself, *I now have six new legs, four new wings, a new head, two new eyes, new antennas, new stomach and intestines. I am a new complex flying creature.*

When the sun came up on the eighth day, I had an exciting adventure ahead. First, I started pushing my way out of the chrysalis. I was through with it for good! In about 30 seconds I was out. I filled my beautiful wings with fluid from my abdominal muscles. My wings were fully inflated in 15 minutes. I was a sight to see! My two large front wings had a span of four inches from tip to tip. *But do they work?* I thought nervously. My apprehension floated away as I moved my wings up and down in the warm sun. "Boy, it sure feels good to be alive. I now can see all the colors of the things that God has made. I can tell whether or not certain flowers have plenty of nectar by seeing the ultraviolet color reflected from the flowers. I can smell flowers I was unable to smell before. I can taste flower nectars I had not been able to taste before. I can fly away wherever I wish and even fast enough to escape from some of my enemies. It's great to be a monarch butterfly!"

Joe had been following this process with his camera. He said, "Monica, how you have changed! You look so beautiful! You have truly been given a special gift from God." This was the first time I had been able to see my friend clearly. He was a handsome boy with a kind face that seemed to be all smiles right now. I somehow knew he loved me and wouldn't hurt me. We became good friends. Joe and I knew this was a special relationship. A friend is to be cherished.

At first I spent several days just going from one kind of flower to another. I tasted the different kinds of nectars found in the flowers. *Great*, I thought, *I'm sure glad I don't have to eat just milkweed anymore but now I can eat a variety of foods. Won't I have fun tasting all the flowers along the meadow?* I am now a full-grown adult monarch butterfly! I am enjoying every minute of my life that God has given me. I hope you are enjoying the life that God has given you, too.

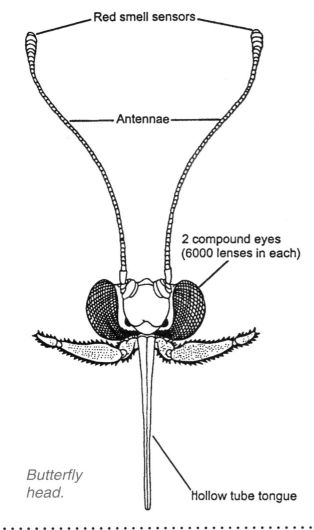

Butterfly head.

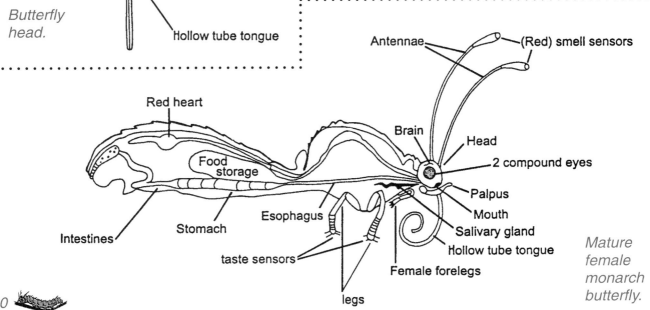

Mature female monarch butterfly.

My Trip to Mexico

By October 1, I was feeling that I should begin my journey to the mountains east of Mexico City where my parents wintered. Joe knew I might leave any day so he picked me up and said "Monica, I won't hurt you. I just want to write your name on a small piece of paper and glue it to one of your forewings. Then when you return from Mexico, I'll know it's you." He made my name tag small enough so it didn't bother my flying. It was nice knowing I would have a friend waiting for me.

The next morning, I noted the time when the sun came up. From this information I could tell how far north I was. I then compared my local time with the time set on my internal reference clock and located how far west I was from Halifax, Nova Scotia, Canada. Then I set my Mexico wintering site location information into my navigational computer. The output of my computer located inside me told me to set a course angle of southwest at 234 degrees. Inside my head and chest regions were particles of an iron compound (ferric oxide)

Monica says goodbye to Joe.

Monica plans her journey south.

that I used to detect the direction of the earth's magnetic field. This helped me to determine my direction, or course angle, to my destination in Mexico.

I started my journey toward the southwest on October 1. It was a beautiful sunny day. The birds were singing, and the smell of gorgeous flowers was everywhere. I enjoyed sipping the sweet nectar from different flowers as I traveled along. I normally traveled about 50 miles per day. Therefore, it would take me about 60 days to travel 3,000 miles to Mexico where my parents wintered in the mountains. I usually traveled only during the ten hours of daylight. Thus, I would travel at an average speed of 5 miles per hour. I could fly at a top

speed of 30 miles per hour if no tail wind was helping me to fly faster. With tail winds I sometimes flew at speeds near 50 miles per hour. That is as fast as cars that drive along the highways.

I was enjoying the trip south for the first two weeks when suddenly I had a bad experience. A man named Mike caught me in his butterfly net when I was busy sipping nectar deep in a large flower. Mike collected butterflies and took them home and killed them and then mounted them on a board. Mike put me in a basket and shut the lid of the basket tight so I couldn't get out. He then put the basket in the trunk of his car and drove off. It was dark and hot in that trunk

Monica escapes!

and I was scared. We traveled all day for miles. Finally, the car stopped and Mike opened the trunk door. It was now getting dark outside. Mike was getting several other things out of the car and then he picked up the basket with me inside. As Mike took a step forward in the dark he didn't see the big rock near the pathway and he stumbled and fell down on the ground. My basket hit the rock hard and the basket lid popped open and I flew out of the basket. Wow! Was I glad to escape Mike. That was a close one! God was watching over me that day!

I flew to the farthest tree I

could see in the dim light, and to its highest branch. How far I was taken off course from my direction to Mexico I could not tell until morning when the sun came up. I was very hungry because I had not eaten all day, but I had to wait until morning so I could see better. I thanked God that I had escaped from Mike's basket.

The next morning, I determined my

location by noting the time the sun came up over the horizon and comparing my local time with my reference time. I had been moved 500 miles west of my previous morning's time. I checked my navigation computer which gave me the new course angle or direction I must take to get to my original Mexico destination. There was still time to get to Mexico because I had started my trip early in the fall.

23

My First Storm

Soon I smelled perfume from some flowers. My two smelling sensors on the ends of my two antennas helped me to determine the direction I must go to get to them. There were more flower perfume molecules coming in my right antenna smelling sensor so I flew to the right. As I got closer to the flowers two miles away I began to see where they were. The flowers were in the little valley over the next hill. I flew higher to get a better look and sure enough, there they were. There were several kinds of flowers: dandelions, butter-cups, daisies, and mum blossoms. I sped up to get there quicker. I was very hungry. Finally, I reached the flowers and enjoyed myself thoroughly. I saw many other butter-flies feeding on the flowers, including mon-archs, too. These other monarchs were also heading for the wintering sites in Mexico.

With my stomach full, I turned myself in the direction of Mexico. I could see mountains in the distance that I must fly over, but that was no problem. I could fly 12,000 feet high if I had to, and most moun-tains in America are less than 10,000 feet. I usually stayed close to the ground even when I flew over mountains, but sometimes I flew high to see the pretty view below. As I flew over mountains I could see herds of deer, some wild goats, and beautiful fir and pine trees. There were streams of running water with little puddles of water nearby. I stopped several times to get a drink in one of these small water puddles. It sure was nice to be able to fly and see all these beautiful sights from high up in the sky. Have you ever been in an airplane and seen how it looks high in the sky? I hope so — it's lots of fun to fly! Don't you wish you could fly?

I finally got over the mountains and down into a nice green grass-covered valley. There were a lot of flowers to sip nectar from in this valley. I sipped nectar until sunset and then flew to a high tree and folded my wings straight up. I slept all night in that position and rested awaiting the dawn of the morning.

The next morning when I woke up I sensed that the air pressure was decreas-ing. This told me a storm was coming and I'd better seek a good place to protect myself from the rain and strong winds. I flew in a wide circle and measured the pressure as I went along. I could tell from the pressure measurements that the storm was coming from the north, so I began flying south as fast as I could. For a while I flew higher to see the direction from which the storm clouds were coming. Then I flew even faster south in the opposite direction. I saw other monarchs and birds flying south also. Birds can also tell when storms are coming by noting that the pressure is de-creasing. We were all trying to escape the fury of the storm. Finally, as night ap-proached, I was getting tired. My heart had been beating faster all day and my muscles were tired. I knew I must quickly find a good shelter. Suddenly I saw a large group of pine trees about a mile away. I arrived just as the sun was going down. There were hundreds of other monarch butterflies

Monica fights the storm!

on these pine trees. I got in the middle of a group of these monarchs and we all folded up our wings in an upward position to protect us from the rain as much as possible. Clustering together helped us to keep warm and also helped to protect us from the strong winds. We always gathered on the leeward side of the tree where the wind was not blowing as fast. It helps to have friends in times of trouble, don't you think?

The wind was beginning to blow fast as the night drew on. I could feel the wind vibrating my antennas and blowing my wings and hairs back and forth. The rain began to fall and I felt the drops falling on my wings. It's a good thing my wings are

somewhat waterproof. They are made up of 1.4 million scales (see wing scale photo on page 27). Each wing scale is filled with air which makes my wings more buoyant, or floatable, so I can fly better and survive rainstorms easier. However, I can't withstand long periods of rain, because my wings will eventually get water-soaked so that I can't fly. I could see the flashes of lighting in the distance and prayed it wouldn't strike me. I could also smell the pollen of many flowers as the storm winds blew my way.

By morning the storm had stopped and the sun was shining once more. Boy, was I glad!

Attacked by Birds

After the storm was over I used the sun's position to locate myself again. The storm had blown me off course by 12 miles. I used my navigational computer to determine which direction I had to go to get to my Mexico wintering site. By the way, even on cloudy days I can see where the sun is, but humans can't.

I started traveling toward Mexico again. Things were going well for several weeks and I was enjoying the trip. However, the following week I had another bad experience.

I was enjoying the day, minding my own business, when suddenly I heard a flurry of beating wings. Much to my dismay, I looked to my right and saw two very hungry birds flying towards me. I overheard one say "Which wing do you want?" Obviously, they had me in mind for their lunch!

Without a moment's hesitation, I flew as fast as I could toward a dense bush area doing acrobatics along the way. They followed closely. One of the birds tore off a small portion of my rear wing before I escaped in the dense bush. I hid for several hours until I was sure it was safe to leave. It made me feel very sad to see one of the birds eat a fragment of another monarch butterfly, but I was happy that the bird got sick and vomited up what he had eaten. I've always been glad that God made monarchs so that birds get sick when they eat us. God did this to protect me. Monarchs eat milkweed in their caterpillar stage which is poisonous to most birds. There are two kinds of birds that can eat monarchs. Even at that, they only eat certain portions of our bodies that doesn't make them sick. Again, I thanked God for saving my life. Has God saved your life?

Birds chase Monica!

South of the Border

Now that the birds were gone, I began my journey to Mexico again. The weather was becoming warmer as I traveled southwestward. Although it was tempting to linger and play in the warm sunshine, I knew I must hurry to my wintering site if I were to arrive in time to lie dormant for the winter, or hibernate, for four months. I needed this restful hibernation time to prepare me for the long 3,000-mile journey back to my home in Canada. I now traveled faster than normal and ate less nectar. Finally, I could see the high mountains where my father and mother wintered. The first half of my journey was over. There are about 13 different sites where monarchs winter in the neo-volcanic mountains west of Mexico City.

On December 25 my navigational sensors led me to the *exact tree* on which my parents wintered. How did I find the same tree my parents were on? Only God in His infinite wisdom knows. I personally think that should be one of the seven wonders of the world! It was a tall pine tree located on a mountain 11,000 feet high. There were over 300 million monarchs wintering on these 13 sites. My site had about 50,000 monarchs. My tree was host to about 2,000 monarchs. We clustered together with our wings folded upward to

Butterfly wing scales, magnified x 22.

Monarchs clustering, magnified x 0.3.

protect us from the rains, winds, and cold nights that we experienced. The temperature at night was near freezing. However, during the day it got warm enough at 10 degrees centigrade so I could fly to a nearby flower and sip some nectar and drink a little water from a stream nearby. The cold night air enabled us to live a longer life because we didn't need to eat or drink much and our bodies rested a lot.

Many people came to visit us from Mexico, the United States, and other parts of the world. It took many years of tagging monarch butterflies to find out where we winter every year. There is a similar migration in South America. It was fun to watch the people utter their "Wow's" and "Oh's" in complete amazement when they saw so many millions of monarchs on these trees. Hope you can visit our wintering site someday. Will you?

Female monarch, magnified x 1.4.

Male monarch, magnified x 1.4.

My Journey Back Home

On May 1 I felt the urge to go back home to Halifax, Nova Scotia. I had rested four months and was ready to return. I missed Joe and I couldn't wait to see him. It was good to feel the warm sun again and drink the sweet nectar from the many flowers that were now blooming everywhere. The northeast direction took me through many interesting states with all kinds of landforms and vegetation. The scenery was breathtaking. Other monarch butterflies I spoke with said they were going to go to different states. Some were going to Alabama, some to Virginia, and others to all the states east of the Rocky Mountains. However, home for me will always be Nova Scotia, Canada. There I will find Indian Creek, the beautiful stream of water where my mother laid the egg that was to become me. There's no place like home.

Monica and Mark.

I Meet Mark, My Mate

After eight weeks, on July 1, I met a special monarch butterfly. His name was Mark. He was going back to Nova Scotia, also. We became great friends. He would circle around me and spray his perfume at me that smelled like many sweet flowers. I liked this perfume and would always get near him when he sprayed it at me. The 600 eggs inside my egg chamber were growing into maturity and were now ready to receive a sperm so that other monarchs could be born. Mark gave me some sperm and I stored them in my sperm pouch. I began to attach my eggs with sperm in them to milkweed leaves as my mother did. I attached one egg at a time on each milkweed leaf as I continued to travel home. I was getting tired and my wings were pretty badly worn out from the 6,000-mile journey. I finally arrived in Halifax, Nova Scotia, Canada, on September 1. I attached my last egg to the same milkweed plant that I was born on. I had arrived home, at last my journey was over, and it felt good to be home again!

When Joe saw me he was so glad that he cried tears of joy. My small name tag was still on my wing. Joe was concerned for me when he saw the condition of my wings. "My poor little Monica," Joe said. "Your wings are so tattered and torn. Your beautiful coloring has faded from orange to an almost yellow color. The black border of your wings now looks gray and your white spots are a dirty creamy-white color." Joe noticed that there were holes in my wings from the long 6,000-mile round trip. He said, "Here is some honey for you to eat, my little Monica." It tasted so good and the honey gave me the extra energy I needed. It was great to be with my friend in the place that I call home.

As the next 30 days passed by I watched my last egg turn into a caterpillar, then a chrysalis, and then into a beautiful wonderful, girl monarch butterfly. Joe called her Mona. We had a wonderful time. She was beautiful and full of energy. She left for Mexico on October 1, just one year and 30 days after I had left for Mexico. Joe tagged Mona and waited for her return. We waved goodbye as she took off for the adventure of her life, just as I had done.

I hope you remember all the wonderful things about the monarch butterflies that you have read in this book. It is also my wish that you will help to preserve our lives on this great planet we call Earth.

Joe's Final Words

Monica died on October 2. She had lived for one year and one month. She lived a long and beautiful life for a butterfly. Most butterflies live for only about two months. It made me sad to watch her become tired and faded, but my mother said that we are all appointed a time to die. She said it is as much a part of living as being born. I was glad that we had our time together. I promised her I would be as good a friend to Mona as I had been to her. At the very end of her life, she curled up on my palm and her wings fluttered one last time. I put her dead body into a nice match box coffin and buried her in my backyard under an old apple tree that she had loved. I put a cross over her grave and played taps for her with my bugle. I think Monica would have liked that.

I will always remember Monica, my favorite butterfly. Not only was she my trusted friend, but I have learned a valuable lesson I would like to share with each of you. God designed her to show me how great a Designer He is. Monica had so much detail and precision that it boggled my mind. Her design also showed me that as God transformed the blind caterpillar inside the chrysalis into a beautiful flying butterfly, so He can also transform my soul and my mortal body into an immortal soul and body to live with Him for all eternity. I hope you believe in God and are trusting Him for your eternal destiny. Someday we can also "fly away."

Monica's final, peaceful resting place.